I0756420

FINISHING LINE PRESS
www.finishinglinepress.com

Orgone Accumulator

poems by

Andre F. Peltier

Finishing Line Press
Georgetown, Kentucky

Orgone Accumulator

For Solstice, Aiden, Jules, and Hugo

ISBN 979-8-89990-502-5 First Edition

Publisher: Leah Huete de Maines
Editor: Christen Kincaid
Cover Art: Craig Dionne
Author Photo: Sara Peltier
Cover Design: Elizabeth Maines McCleavy

Order online: www.finishinglinepress.com
also available on amazon.com

Author inquiries and mail orders:
Finishing Line Press
PO Box 1626
Georgetown, Kentucky 40324
USA

Contents

Part I: Barbed Wired Days

In the Arena of the Alligator

"Well, I'm goin' down to Florida
Get some sand in my shoes" [1]

We loaded the army green
Pinto wagon
& headed south
for the land of orange blossoms
& coconut palms.
We saw Rock City
& the birth place of Davy Crockett,
but our mission
was to find the warmth of the sun
on the white sunshine shores
of the white sunshine state.
In Fort Myers
we ate burgers and watched
Cary Grant catch a fish
with his bare hands,
but he never gave it a half-nelson.
He never attempted a suplex
on that South Pacific island.
After Cheerios
& hard-boiled eggs,
we passed through
Bonita Springs, Naples,
Marco Junction in search of
pastel landscapes
& Art Deco beaches.

We never heard the whistle
of that train from New York City.
We never saw that cocaine sunrise
over the cocaine sands of Miami.

East of Okeechobee
we got lost in Big Cypress.
Driving those muddy two-tracks
& the reed ensconced paths
of the ancient Seminole Nation,
our ancient Pinto
was axle-deep in turtles,
snail kites, marsh rabbits.
Asking directions

at a gas station,
we drank Dr. Peppers
& sampled the local jerky,
but out back was something special.
I was seven years old,
too young to be wandering alone
in the black water swamps,
but I wandered alone
& found the soul of old Florida.
As the river is the heart
of the land pumping life-blood
water through arteries
of peninsular wet-lands,
the soul of a state
is hidden in
its tourist traps.

He never heard the whistle
Of that train for New York City
He never saw that golden sunrise
Over his ancestral sands of Miami

Behind that gas station,
a grizzled man with
grizzled teeth
waited to put on his show.
Three generations of that
Osceola family
paid their bills
& paid their dues
in the arena of the alligator.
The arena of the prehistoric beast.
The trick is to fight a big one:
the muscle mass makes them
slower and less flexible.
Before De Soto, before Ponce de Leon,
his family were royalty:
kings, queens, princes.
I watched the Duke of Chokoloskee,
with his scars and filth, roll a gator,
catch a tooth in his forearm,
and pin it for a ten count.
We got back in the old Pinto
& headed further down
The Tamiami Trail
as the arterial swamp pumped us
towards the shore.

West of Texarkana

In Northeastern Texas,
on the prairie between
Paris and Texarkana,
the sun was setting
on the Year of our Lord
2011.
Lost on a muddy two-track,
we saw an enormous buck
silhouetted against
the rising stars
of New Years dusk.
Abandoned Fords, Buicks,
& Toyotas
rested in an open field
w/ brush and weeds
towering through their trunks
& hoods.
Left ajar by past owners
or forced ajar by time
& rust,
the trunks & hoods revealed
the vacant void of history.
Abandoned trailers,
washing machines, & tires
grew where the rattlesnakes
& rabbits once played
their endless game of tag.
We turned the rental car around
to head back in time
for beer, & fireworks,
hoping to make it through
the soft sand, the deep ruts
when we saw their eyes
flash in the headlights.
Glowing white & hollow,
a dozen spaniels blocked our route.
They'd been left like
the Fords, the Buicks,
& the Toyotas,
like the tires & washing
machines.

Once well-fed & tame,
they lived off the land.

These dogs,
in touch more with
the hidden coyotes
& razorback killers
than with their housebroken
brethren,
were learning the ways
of their wolfen ancestors.
They stood their ground
as if to say:

"This land is ours again.
This North Texas waste
belongs to North Texas
wretchedness.
Like the tires & Toyotas,
we now make the calls."

Joshua Tree

The golden rays
of southern California sunset
glowed through southern
California smog
as we turned east
at Barstow in
a borrowed car.
We turned east
on that two-lane black-top
over borrowed Mojave land.
Just past a truck stop
where we loaded down
with Doritos, root beer,
Little Debbie Swiss Cake Rolls,
we passed a Joshua Tree.
We were our own Wheeler Expedition
surveying the land
and gathering specimens
for future study.
George Englemann saw the trees
and remembered his family bible.
Those Mormons too,
saw the trees.
And Joshua raised his hands
to guide the conquering Israelites
through Canaan,
to victory over their desert foes.
In Needles, w/ tacos for breakfast
and tacos in our tank,
we remembered those early days
3,000 years ago.
In the court of Josiah,
they remembered the hands of Joshua,
outstretched and strong.
At Needles,
we used the yucca palm
to guide our expedition up the hills
beyond those feral mules
to Oatman, Kingman, Seligman.
But before George Wheeler,
the Mojave was rattlesnake land.
The ancient Mojave
had rattlesnake visions
and moon flower dreams.

We ate our Doritos
and made good time.
The two-lane black-top
opened into I-40 freedom;
that Barstow Joshua Tree
in our rearview mirror
and in our parched
Yuman
dust.

See Rock City

I go to the woods at sun-up,
walk barefoot through
frost and fallen leaves.
Wide-eyed, I
watch the rise over canyons
and the frozen Georgia hills.
Further south,
iron-rich soil
baked by iron-rich sun
nurtures cotton fields,
peach trees, peanut plantations.
Fields, trees, plantations
bring the riches of the world
to Waycross, Savannah,
and Macon,
but the frost in the northern hills
just freezes my dirty toes.
No longer do we meet a power
there in those hills,
no longer can we worship
the chilly Tennessee Valley.
Divorced from romantic feelings
of oneness,
atop Lookout Mountain
we see seven states,
and seven states only.
And I go to the woods at sun-up,
send my dirty toes down
into rocky earth,
attempting to make those
old connections,
attempting to fill my own private
Tallulah Gorge,
nurtured by the
iron-rich sun.

Down the Barbed Wire Highway

Northern Arizona
through desert of dreams
Kingman from Needles
and beyond.
We haggled for a bed,
ate tacos for breakfast
and set out to find
the south rim.
We set out for
a trip back in
time.

In Oatman town
the road skirted the cliffs,
climbed the narrow pass.
Rusted barbed wire
marked our progress
and the empty mines
yawned of John Carter & Johnny Moss.
Singing songs of Carole Lombard,
we were haunted by the ghost of
Billy Ray Flour.
Oatman,
then as now,
the last living Ghost town.

We'd already
witnessed the ghosts of
Cisco.
The prairie dogs of
Cisco
filled Rte. 128
North of Moab
before we found
Goblin Valley and
the fabled
canyons of Cassidy.

We followed the barbed wire
to the Sno-Cap
before turning north at Williams,
home of Old Bill and the Roadrunner.

At our campsite
we watched the elk.
The ravens held the gifts
like so much sugary cereal,
and we cast our gaze
at the past...
and the past cast its gaze back
at us.
Rock layers:
The Cocconino Sandstone,
the Hermit Formation,
the Redwall Limestone.
The Paleozoic parapets piercing to
white water.
We threw
stones and our voices
echoed through the chasm.

"Ai Chihuahua,"
the river sounded back.

Across Pigeon Key

Across Pigeon Key
and Little Duck,
there runs a highway
over the Gulf.
Over the Moser Channel.
In the old days,
the train bridge
carried passengers
and freight
to the end of the
continent.
Before that,
it was simply
Henry Flagler's
fantastical fever-dream.
To unite the mainland
with the Holy Keys.
To unite angels and anglers
with the holy tarpon,
grouper, snapper, cobia.

We crossed The Seven Mile Bridge
going southwest,
leaving the land behind
for another world.
In those days,
the bridge swung out
for passing vessels:
cruise ships, freighters,
trawlers with their nets
full to bursting,
and so we waited
for over an hour
on a thin piece of asphalt
in the middle of
white rushing waves.
We waited and watched
wandering about, gazing
over the edge.
Sharks and stingrays
navigating the shallows
near the supports.
They cut through crystal waters
not unlike how we cut through

the tiny keys,
sand bars really
with a tuft of grass
and a coconut palm.
Outpost to outpost,
an artery pumping tourists
to sun and surf,
rum and freedom.
Outpost to outpost,
the Overseas Highway
offers a glimpse of
Hemingway,
a glimpse of Tennessee Williams
and his southern charm.
As the Seven Mile Bridge
swung back,
we got in the car,
knowing our time was short.
How long will the highway
survive?
Another hurricane, another
mad tantrum?
Another day
at least.

Above New River Gorge

Up the mountain,
to forgotten cemetery,
rusted water-tower,
we dragged late-model
Dodge Dart.
A tight squeeze,
that car made it
through the narrowest
of over-grown erosion.
The gaping ravine
held life once
and would again.
We baked
in the sun.

An hour later,
the rains came,
but we came first.
We made that
back-bumper bounce
atop those pock-marked hills.
Alone below that tower,
the cloudless sky
stood still
as we made it run,
born again: anew
and alone.
Below that tower,
we smiled in
the sun.

Gaspé Peninsula

> "Dans les grandes cites, dans les bois, sur les grêves,
> Ton image flottera dans mes rêves,
> O mon Canada, bien aimé." [1]

Roadside ovens
with warm, crusty baguette.
Wine for the adults,
grape juice for the children.
Open expanse,
from Chic-Choc highlands
of caribou and Jacques-Cartier,
to rolling grasses.
Over to those steep cliffs
before falling to
The Gulf and Newfoundland,
to Cardiff and Cork.

Wading to Rocher Percé
before the tide came in.
Like a beacon,
the phantom rock floats
on the waves warning
freighters of rough waters ahead.
We heed the signal,
rolling up our jeans
before climbing,
falling, splashing
back to the mainland.

And the highway hugs
the coastline between
limestone wall
and expansive deep.
There, out the window,
you could reach and rub
the sounding humpbacks.
Laughing in the waves,
they too splashed back
to safety before their
great migration
to tropical
playgrounds.

Leave Only Mufflers

Like Clark Griswold,
every year my old man
would load us into
the Peltier family automobile
and haul us cross-country.
That olive green Ford Pinto
ate up the road while guzzling gas
and breaking down.
The clutch failed
rolling through the Smokies.
The radiator made it to within
an hour of Orlando.
We found a garage,
ate garlic bread and ravioli,
and missed our chance
to experience The Tea Cups
and Mr. Toad's Wild Ride.
Annapolis, 1984,
we watched Olympic soccer:
France (the eventual champions),
Chile, and Qatar. Chilean fans
chanting "Chi, Chi, Chi... Le Le, Le...
Chi-Le, Chi-Le, Chi-Le!"
are tattooed in my memory,
but with a crowded car,
the old man accidently left me behind,
I wandered those streets
for hours, alone, scared, in tears.
One time,
heading north through Georgia,
the brakes went and my old man
had to reach Michigan
by drafting behind semis,
downshifting, and squeezing
the parking brake.
It was something to behold.
From Macon to Toledo,
it was something to behold.

Boats too, were part of Dad's itinerary.
Bar Harbor to Yarmouth,
with Burt Lancaster, Kirk Douglass,
and those holy slot machines.
Whale watching in Boston,

it rained, we saw no whales,
and Elizabeth got sea sick,
threw up over the stern.
Fishing off the coast of Sarasota
for grouper, snook, snapper.
A guy hooked a sea turtle
and we had to pull in our hooks.
Crew thought it a shark,
the turtle was endangered;
they had to cut the line.
Twice we steamed out to Fort Dade
and climbed around the ruins
as they slowly fell to the bottom
of the Gulf of Mexico.
And on the ferry to Liberty Island,
I saw my first breast.
A young woman in a loose tank top...
hairy pits, hard nipples,
braless.

Those summers,
no park east of the Mississippi was safe:
state, national, amusement...
like the Griswold's,
we wrecked them all.
I collected mouse-ear hats, coon-skin caps,
little imported totem poles.
Taking only souvenirs
and leaving only mufflers
in our wake.

Part II: The Great Basin

Someone Else's Stars

The sun is our center
bringing light and life.
Painted on the walls
of Lascaux caves,
the sun illuminates
the bulls
and the Magdalenian
artists.
Worshiped by naked pagans
in mid-winter dance,
her eight-minute flicker
renews the soul
and reminds the senses
of calming spring.
"Prepare to plow and sow,"
says the sun on the Winter
Solstice.
"Prepare for another
940 million km,"
she echoes through the void.
Days grow longer
as the axis allows
the angled gleam.
The axis allows those
seasonal shifts.
The axis on which we spin,
it is necessary and it is also
our center.
Not the sun only,
but our rotation too
permits us.
We spin and spin
in clumsy, drunken laughter
as those 940 million km
again blink by.
We spin and spin
but rarely stop to consider.
We are the center;
we gaze to the heavens
and project myth onto stars.

When Gan De sat
cataloguing the sky,
when Gan De saw
the four moons of Jupiter,
he understood the mysteries
of the void.
Gan De,
for a moment anyway,
glanced the vastness of
possibilities.
The vastness of the solar system;
the vastness of imagination.
The return gaze was
always-already
present in his Warring State.
Before the Spring,
before the Autumnal Era,
he saw through to the depths
of truth,
and it was out there
seeing through to him.

In The Book of Fixed Stars,
al-Sufi fixed the heavens.
A millennium ago,
al-Sufi picked up his glass
and cast his gaze starward.
A blur above Yemeni skies
with its obscured haze
and rotating lights,
the Large Magellanic Cloud
gazed back
and discovered the Arabian
Peninsula.
A nebulous sphere
gazed back
and discovered
al-Sufi al-so.

Corsono sat with pen
and glass bringing science to
Catalonian Jews.
Illuminating benighted lives;
illuminating the frum
Rabbi of Barcelona,
Valencia, Sicily.

The stars were their center.
Not the Star of David only,
but the twinkling darkness too.
They knew not of Proxima b
or Bernard's Star.
They knew only their piety
and their prayers.
Proxima b knew not of
their Catalonian observers.

And what of the folks traveling
around Proxima b?
What of the folks who watch
Bernard's Star rise and set
each day?
They, too, look skyward.
Like Gan De, al-Sufi,
Corsono,
they, too, gaze
into the vastness.
When they see our sun,
twinkling in the sable
field of dreams,
they connect its dot
to other twinkles.
Giving shape to the shapeless
expanse, we are
but a shoulder
or a hoof in
someone else's
stars.

Still Life w/ Locomotives

And in Paris,
there is the Musée d'Orsay.
Housing the world's largest
collection of Impressionist art,
it opened in 1986
and has been hailed
as one of the best
in the world.
The Beaux-Arts train station
on the Left Bank is, itself,
a masterpiece.
No longer do those locomotives
chug and puff,
no longer will we see
the smoke and steam
escape to the sky.
The engines, with their
legs open wide
and their faces
divorced from their bodies,
no longer lay in repose
along the river.

The trains would arrive
on schedule every day,
every hour.
Off to Marseilles, or Lyon
or Barcelona,
the trains would
chug chug chug
out of the station
with business men
and tourists and young American
women
looking for husbands
and truth.
Up to Calais,
they could almost see
the towering cliffs,
the towering bee hives.
The club cars crammed
with Londoners
ready to cross the channel
and settle back at home

with tea and drizzle
and eel pie.

From Dover,
those Blue Bloods would
bounce north,
never thinking of the future
or what would become
of their beloved Parisian nights.
They drank to the legs
and stockings in cabaret shadows.
They bought little Eiffel Towers
to give to their sons
upon return.
They passed under the
Arc de Triomphe
never casting a gaze
on the grave.

The first flame
to burn eternally
since the lights of the virgins
were extinguished so many
years before.
The Unknown Soldier
below the cobblestone paths,
naked without his
gas-mask or his L&B 8mm.
He lays on guard,
ready to rise from the grave
when the nation
should need him next.
When the nation should need
Protection from
invading hoards.
Did those American girls
visit Les Invalides?
Did they pay tribute to
Henri Bertrand?
He carried the corpse
back from St. Helena
but was overlooked by those girls...
a better husband is surely out there
riding those rails,
walking those gardens,
drinking cognac and coffee.

In the halls:
Manet, Cézanne,
Gauguin.
Our celebrated masters.
Seurat's Circus spins
as the gleaners glean.
The Source,
with longing eyes: starry and pure,
watches and wonders
as tourists wander
overwhelming walls.
When the Paris Commune
held sway,
d'Orsay was an exhibit too...
an exhibit of the here and
now.

Today, we enter and
look back with calm
nostalgia at the niceties
of history's constant
chugga chugga chug.

Goodnight, Taj Mahal

Deep below earth, clay and sand,
deep below roots and aquifers,
it lies in wait. Like that silent coyote
stalking her white-tailed deer
through the brush,
it waits patiently
and with the purity of Assisi.
When Francis of Assisi
preached to the birds, the rams,
the donkeys, that Harlem backbeat
was waiting. The rhythm of India
and the echoes of conch.
Where Mumtaz sleeps beside
Shah Jahan, where ivory towers
watch ivory crowns
waiting behind ivy walls.
Like Cardinals, like a lighthouse
on the rocky cliffs of Maine,
they watch and wait.
From Hibbing down to Cairo
and from Cairo to old Cave-in-Rock.
Where the Nolichucky waters
run crisp and clear,
the man in the Panama hat strums
and sings and knows he'll never fall.

Goodnight, Taj Mahal

Icebergs in Midwestern winter chill
come faster and faster comes
the wind, the snow,
the flying leaves over fallow fields.
Empty snowflakes watch
and watch with banjo strings
the chestnut air of November.
And when the man cakewalks into town,
when the tuba sets the pace,
we see stars and the eclipse,
we dance the dance of
aurora borealis,
and remember Assisi's dance.
Who but the saint of Italian imagination
could free the leper's corroded soul?
And as his hands bled, ours bled too.

Light passes through
our collective palms,
and light passes through
the chestnut air of November,
but it sure don't mean
a natural thing.
The man in the Panama hat
descends steps of Eremo Delle Carceri,
wanders with Paul who was Saul.

Goodnight, Taj Mahal

On the road to Damascus,
Paul who was Saul fell blind
from his mount.
He fell blind from the light of conversion.
In the shadows
of the snowy Lebanon Range,
he waited for the rhythm of India
and he waited for direction.
Sailing to Puteoli,
he waded through the waves of Malta
and dragged chains while anchors sank.
Paul prayed to Christ
and Rhea Silva.
Twelve centuries battered by Euroclydon winds,
twelve centuries of eastward glances,
and Francis bled like Christ.
The palms of humanity
split open and wept their tears
of blood onto Assisi's white roses.
Blood pumped to the rhythm
of blackest Indian night.
But Mary of Bethany,
don't you weep for your brother.
Don't weep for the man
in the Panama hat.

Goodnight, Taj Mahal

In train stations, barns,
Down dead-end streets,
Paul's gale force winds lie in wait.
Sleepers on station benches,
entrenched in quilted newsprint,
wait for winter winds to cease.

They wait for the rhythm of India
and echoes of the conch
to resonate in marble halls
and resonate with the riders
of the world.
And in Il Buco del Diavolo,
Assisi slept with Italian sparrows,
the Italian wall lizards, the Italian bleak.
They kept each other happy,
winsome and warm in the devil's hole.
And the wall lizard freed
the leper's empty soul.
Like a free song falling
on freedom's sloppy ears,
we fly from tree to tree.
All while the man
in the Panama hat
rode off on a broke-down mule,
so slow and small.

Goodnight, Taj Mahal

In dilapidated barns of Commerce,
Cornelia, and Dillard,
in the shells of burned-out houses,
in dark alleys filled with the ghosts
of razor-wielding cut-throats,
the western wind whips and whines.
It winds around the seven Roman hills.
Where Rhea Silva met Mars
and her Apennine twins
were suckled by the Etruscan she-wolf,
the western wind reverberates
with the melodies of India and Harlem.
When Tallulah Gorge split open and sang,
the winds sang too.
They blew to dark
Tuckahoe caves of Inwood Hill.
The man in the Hawaiian shirt
counted one hundred and twenty-five
words per stanza,
knowing there would be no more
and absolutely no less.
The grey-bearded man
in the Panama hat
rode a mule that never missed

the water in his stall.

Goodnight, Taj Mahal

In the hour of salt and snow,
a dash of flavor that was Edith
puts finger to lips,
secreting that melody of the wind.
Hushed and hidden,
the melody lies forgotten.
The salt of Edith spills
across the cities of the plains
and across the great Ghor of Jordan.
Towards the Dead Sea
it runs carrying
the melody of the wind.
Towards the boot-heal
of Ionian quietude, it runs.
The silent spine where Assisi slept
keeps mum the riddle of Lot.
From Clingman's Dome to Baldpate
and from Middleberry
to the blood of Killdeer Mountain
where Sitting Bull, Gull,
and Inkaduta stood strong.
Halleluiah, the man in the Panama hat
rings clear those new, new Easy Rider Blues:
long, loud, and eternal,
forever to call.

Goodnight, Taj Mahal

We fertilize those fallow fields
with our gaze,
carry the nexus of the universe
between our shoulder blades.
Beating on his ribcage
like a talking drum,
beating on windows
like hailstones flying from those fields
bewildered and naked,
he's done the dense dance of ennui
weighed down by lonely boredom.
Every hour counts its holocaust
in tiny ashbins of truth and yesterday.
In the gelatoria, the salumeria,

the bowels of the forno,
they pray to Assisi for guidance.
They call to the saints to intervene.
They climb those storied steps
to Trinità del Monti
and gaze through opened palms.
Who was that masked man recycling blues
and wearing his Panama hat,
emissary from the violent first day?
From the crying eyes
of Charles de Gaul?

Goodnight, Taj Mahal

From those crying eyes
of Charles de Gaul,
we count days with each tear-lined cheek.
When Hirohito cried his A-Bomb tears
into the A-Bomb ashes
of Hiroshima and Nagasaki,
they washed away the terror of surrender.
And Peter cried bitterly, uncontrollably.
And the tears carved canyons
down Peter's face.
And Jesus wept at the tomb of Lazarus
like mermaids,
like sobbing human seals.
When Assisi received the gift of tears,
he looked east for guidance.
Turning eyes toward Yamuna,
toward The Ganges,
he begged for guidance.
The man with the steel guitar
and the Panama hat
cried his river of love
for big legged women.
He received the gift of tears
for his sins and the sins of the world.
The sins of the world.

Goodnight, Taj Mahal

Robben Island Beach Break

Following the sun
and the rolling surf
to the next great beach.
White sands, the curl,
long boards packed on
foreboding jet planes.
Leaving Los Angeles
for warmer winters,

but there's a moment in
Endless Summer
that raises red flags.
The colorblind beaches
of Apartheid
are dreamlike fantasies.
Never do they mention
the toil.
Never the surf-bums
who only ride the crests
of jail-cell satori.
Around the horn,
they find the wilds,
they find virgin white-caps,
they find the simulacra
of freedom.

But they never carved
the waters of Robben Island.
Sisulu, Sobukwe, Seremane
never dipped their toes
in the warm waters of
Robben Island.
Never did Jacob Zuma
hang ten at Zuma
or on those
colorblind beaches.
It was all beach break on
Robben Island.

And Mike, and Bruce
and Robert deplaned in LA
and never looked back.

Bristlecone Soul

I
Eternity walks the mine fields
of World War III
where the undergod is helpless,
forgotten and forlorn.
The undergod comes up for air
with his snorkel and his spear,
but the altar boys stand at attention
none-the-less.
The altar boys pass out
from the heat and the stress
of holding that giant Bible
for the priests to read.
When they stumble,
they are ushered into the wings
to recover,
to see the light,
to rise in prayer,
to rise in redemption and pain.
And we all wore horse hair shirts
as we recovered from the final quakes,
the final landslides,
the final tsunami.
Our cilices mortified our flesh,
mortified our shameful bristlecone souls.
We raised hands to our little gods
and our horse hair shirts were raised too.
As Eternity walked through
those mine fields,
we watched from atop our pillars.
Like Simeon,
we perch on our pillars.
We look over the scorched Earth and wail.
From atop our pillars,
we watch the undergod cry for help
but go forever unheard.
For thirty-seven years,
our collective vertebrae bend and contort.
Our collective vertebrae dislocate,
but we remain silent.
Our bodies are left for ravens,
vultures, crows as we die
on our pillars and feed
those scavengers while they get

their three square
and we get our repentant one-way tickets
to the bowels of those birds
and the bowels of
the unrepentant earth.

"Who was that horse-haired man?"
they ask, as I ride from town,
lacerations on my back,
blood running down to my toes.
"Who was that horse-haired man?"
they beg to know.
For who could be so pious,
so pure, so at one with the pillar,
the mine fields, the undergods?
I sell the finger-bones
of Belina the Virgin:
free shipping and a digit
can be yours.
Belina the Virgin rode
six white horses when she came.
They say her relics were lost
during the Revolution.
They say the fingers,
her fingers, are not her own.
"How can you sell bones lost in 1789?"
They ask. "How can we have such faith?"
Her head, preserved in a statue,
preserved in Mores Abbey,
will lead us all to that tunnel of faith.
We buy our tickets for
The Tunnel of Faith
and then we neck in the darkness.
In the Tunnel of Faith,
our ship takes on water
and begins its never-ending list.
We bail to no avail
as we take on more and more water.
To bail in the tunnel of Faith,
we drown in our own pretensions.
Necking with Belina the Virgin
as we sink below those foamy waves,
we hold her lucky bones and pray
to those undergods of misfortune,
misunderstanding,
misbehavior.

II

We write, "Trout fishing in America"
1,000x on the chalk boards
of the pancreas.
We sign our names
1,000x for Mr. Nesbit
but end up in principals' offices
none-the-less.
We stare into the camera lens
as Noggin sends us to detention
for transgressions forgotten and unknown.
Juveniles Under God,
we polished the cafeteria, raked the leaves,
emptied the cigarette buckets.
"Is it totally bonus?" Alan asked
as our Kitsman cried,
turned out the lights, and left the building.
"I've had it with you people,"
she rebuked as she ran from the room.
And in the back of that pick-up truck,
the undergods smoked
the dirtiest of the dirt weed,
shared airplane bottles of rum,
and crossed their fingers
in that ever-optimistic way
only the undergods can.
The undergods made a bong
out of Belina the Virgin's skull.
Smoke poured out of her eye sockets
as they remembered their first time
on the beaches of Florida,
on the white beaches of the world.
While we wait for the undergods
to pass that skull around,
"don't bogart that skull, my friend."
We wait for the true history
of our concupiscent lust
to take hold and drive us
into the future of unyielding pain.
We never admit to our sick desires,
our bloodhunger, our unknown relics;
to admit would end the pain.
The virgin endured the pain
so we endure as well.
They tighten the chains around our abdomens,
and we raise up our horsehair shirts

to expose more flesh.
“Thank you, Padre, may I have another?”
we weep as we consent.
We weep as we consent
to the horrors of the pleasure principle
and to the horrors of the principles
of science and mathematics.

The mathematics of the soul
stand to be counted by those fallen saints
and those fallen sinners,
but neither saint nor sinner can manage
the complex calculations
of those trigonometric fantasies.
When Belina the Virgin practiced
her multiplication tables,
she refused to marry,
she refused to join that beast-train
coming ‘round the bend
for all points fire and brimstone.
She dangled like a spider over those fiery pits,
but the undergods held tightly
to her gossamer thread.
She wrote “Trout fishing in America”
1,000x as she dangled over the precipice
and hell’s gaping maw beckoned.
Her phalanges clung to the precipice
but never slipped.
Her phalanges now worth
their weight in gold and platinum.
When you buy her fingers,
you ensure your everlasting salvation.
Place them on your mantel
and wash your bristlecone soul clean.
No blemish on the penitent soul,
no eternal suffering.
The overgods know your
cat ‘o nine tails
did its job
keeping you
warm and
safe.

Out Cimarron Way

Through the abyss of infinite
time and space,
through the fields of joyless
amber grain,
through tumult, turmoil, and tension,
hands waving above
white cap undertows,
waiting for deliverance and a chance
to fill lungs to bursting capacity.
Open up and say, "Nah."
Open up and drink to the lees.
Touch toes and bend knees;
open up and drink to the lees.
Unloose the pets from leash and cage,
unloose the cage from foundations
of freefall galactic mortar.
And the mortars fall on No-Man's Land.
And the mortars fall on the DMZ.
And the mortars fall to crater Kiev, Gaza,
The Cimarron Strip.

In the Oklahoma panhandle,
lawlessness abounds.
In the Oklahoma panhandle,
ten-gallon hats watch sunsets
over Taos and over The Petrified Forrest.
The ten-gallon hats
are themselves petrified.
They are themselves scared to death.
They hide in darkened basements
awaiting the boogeyman.
They disguise themselves as top hats
and let long dead presidents wear them
to see Our American Cousin
at the Ford Theater.
In the Oklahoma panhandle,
the ten-gallon hats drive Fords and Chevys
and rope them doggies
and bust them broncos.
The Cimarron Strip, No-Man's Land,
home of the brave, land that time forgot.
Home of the sauroposeiden
and the tenontosaurus.
And the masked man

on his snow-white steed sings,
"Tenontosaurus, you go to town."
"Tenontosaurus, stay here
and watch the camp tonight."

And Tenonto responds,
"Sure, Kemosabe,
but who will watch out for me?
Who will stand by my side
when the oceans rise,
when the meteorites fall,
when the lowly mammals rise
to rule the world?
Who will go to town then,
Kemosabe?"
And Tenonto asks,
"Who will watch
through the abyss
of time and space?"

Gagarin in the Trees

The ghost of Yuri Gagarin
floats down the hallways
of the International
Space Station.
The resident astronauts,
cosmonauts, uchū-hikō-shi
salute as he slides by.
They tell him their deepest secrets
while flushing their filth
into the void.
"Dear Yuri," they say,
"It's been eight hours since
my last evacuation.
I have eaten two portions of
dehydrated chocolate pudding,
and I spent twenty minutes
on the tread mill.
I really miss morning coffee
overlooking the Hollywood sign
and the Kiselyova Rock.
I miss lazy Saturdays
in my garden."

The vacuum of space
greets the spationauts
and the spationauts wave
to Gagarin while falling
27,000 kilometers per hour.
When the falling station
misses the curve of the Earth
again and again,
the spationaut says
a brief prayer,
thanking the engineers,
those great rangers of
the atomic age.
Claudie Haigneré said
her prayers to Gagarin also,
and in return,
he blessed her saintly
homecoming.

The ghost of Yuri Gagarin
eases around the trees

in my back yard
and climbs the tallest
to get a better view.
He climbs the tallest
to recall his vantage
point in orbit.
The ghost of Yuri Gagarin
returns to Клу́шино
and reminisces with his
Muscovite brethren.
They recall
the good old days.
They wait patiently,
and they see what
the future
holds.

She Showed Me Her Scars

The club was dark,
loud, empty.
Sadness floated
over the tables:
a spectre of lost
innocence.
I sat nursing a Scotch;
she sat nursing her
Newport.
"I've been dancing here
for about six months,"
she said.
I nodded with that absent
urgency she saw every hour.
"I'm from out of town,"
I lied,
"Tomorrow it's back to
Chattanooga."
Her ears perked.
She loved Glenn Miller;
on a family road trip
to the Okefenokee Swamp
when she was seven
she'd seen Rock City.
Those South Georgia
alligators though inspired her.
Razor teeth
and whip-like tails:
power, pain, domination.
The apex predator,
just like her.

Those lonely afternoons,
she silently circles the club:
eyes above the haze,
ready to strike.
"I have a new boyfriend,"
she suddenly said.
He's been showing me things."
An unexpected turn.
"OK, I'll bite.
What do you mean?"
Like those Alligators,
he sliced into her.

Slowly, he slid his hooks
beneath her shoulder blades,
hoisted her on chains
to float like that sadness
over candles and rose-petals.
She lowered the silk straps
of her camisole
to show me the incisions.
Two jagged scabs;
two sets of homemade stitches.
"Touch the cuts,"
she whispered.
"Run your fingers over the scars."
In the refracted light
of the mirror-ball,
my long, unknowing fingers
read the braille of her body.
My Scotch remained
unfinished on that table
as I turned to venture back
into frozen November wind.
An apex predator,
just like her.

Uncle Ebenezer / Uncle Stockhausen

I
I dreamt
I saw Joe Strummer
last night
walking down Main St.
w/ a bottle of brandy
tucked under his chin
like a St. Bernard.
Arm in arm
w/ Frankie Yankovic,
the king of Bavaria:
accordion solo.
Polka.

The Alps rising in the
distance.
Rising against the
onslaught of daybreak.
Rising against the
onslaught of darkest night.

Joe Strummer
w/ a fiddle and a cigarette.

The snow-capped Alps:
Mount Blanc and its
mystical power hiding beyond
the clouds.
It descends from
the ice-gulfs that
gird your
Telecaster.
Zugspitze,
peeking into the heavens.
Joe Strummer
wearing a magnificent
dirndl, flying
aboard a white
falcon,
majestic and ancient.
& where has King Yankovic
gone.

Where have you gone
bringer of the beat?
Do you celebrate
Oktoberfest
in the klouds?
Do you await the long
November?

Who cares for you,
Joe Strummer,
In my dreams
and in the clouds?

At dusk,
the owls swoop
and the fruit bats
feast.
At dusk,
we drink the brandy
we remember the old times.
At dusk we close our eyes &
doze.

II
Beats & rhymes;
A world of sonic
dissonance.

Who was that boy
In sophomore biology?
He handed me
Combat Rock
as the defiant ghetto
of the soul of
William S. Burroughs
welcomed us into his
orgasm starved
metropolis.

Lois & Clark:
Can you read her mind?
Clean lungs and pink panties
& power politics.
Lois & Clark
soar over the city
on the white falcon.

& in the supermarket,
lost and alone,
poking among the
stars.

III
Uncle Ebenezer,
Uncle Stockhausen:
they play games w/
society & in the
helicopter melody
of the sleepless
Sandinista
we crash and burn.
Where are you going
tonight,
Joe Strummer?
I see you,
in the dream of a
common commotion,
sunburst rhythm and
revolution.

You're crossing the
Blue Water Bridge,
road trip to Niagara.
I see you in the halls of
Casa Loma & the
back streets of China Town.
I see you eating
chop suey & egg rolls.
I see you in Niagara
At Ripley's & The Flying Saucer.
I see you atop the
CN Tower
w/ one arm waving
free.

Nobel Laureates
bow as you pass,
but we know better.
On this night of long
Novembers,
you bow to
no one.

Part III: Taproot

Boxing the Compass

"If only that little butterfly could
always flutter before me to show me the way"[1]

I watched a monarch
butterfly,
orange, black, white,
flutter among the coneflowers.
It hovered in the spiderwort
boxing the compass
as it traced its path
back and forth,
back and forth
from bud to bud.
I watched and realized.
Like that monarch,
we are all
boxing the compass.
We all flutter back and forth
looking for a place to land.
Looking for that place of
safety, security.
Looking for a place
to call home.

Upside-Down Skies

For Clara Ibarra

I read an article once
about spiders in a lab.
Some were dosed
with LSD,
others with mescaline.
The mescaline spiders
made webs with geometric
precision:
perfect triangles, exact angles,
laser-straight lines.
The LSD spiders, however,
were different.
Their webs seemed
a chaotic mess.
Gossamer strands akimbo,
the acid webs were everything
we expect from
acid-head
arachnids.

I saw a painting once,
barren trees reflected
in an upside-down sky:
large limbs, small branches,
stately trunks.
They wiggled and shook
like the liquid lines
of those spaced-out
spiders.
I wonder if those spiders saw
the world like that.
Did they know reflected clouds
with flying birds throughout?
Ink-blot atmosphere
folded, doubled,
the perfect field for
perfect hawks.
Perfect lysergic
inspiration.

The Center of Gravity

Two bodies in orbit
Circling and circling
Never meeting until their time
Never meeting until
the destiny of their endless
starlit sky compels them
to entangle their dreams.
Only in orbit can these
bodies stalk in narrowing gyre.
Only in the space of the mind
can they truly become one.
Under milky heavens,
emerging from cosmic
filth of time and
history's somber slop,
in the space of a minute,
the planets form
and awaken
to gaze into each other's eyes.
They awaken to watch
the rising and falling
of a breast.
Inhaling the clear crisp
October night.
The planets carve their initials
in park benches
and in beech tree wilderness.
The planets are locked
in boundless dance.
To the music of the spheres,
they twirl and twirl.
Until their jubilant collapse,
they twirl and twirl.

Waiting for the Sploosh

I: From Scranton to St. Helens

Staring into the vacuum
of wishing well satori.
The penny drops, drops
but never hits bottom.
The penny carries
the unfulfilled dreams
of unfulfilled nations.
Through maize and gourds
and golden autumnal afternoons,
the penny drops
never to hit rock bottom.
With hearing aids and
Whisper 2000s
we squint our ears
to detect the faint clink
of copper on granite.
Never again will we
fold our hands,
bow our heads.
Never again will we
ask God to save the day.
"There is absolutely no
justification—none—
for looting. No justification
for violence."[1] Ah, but he
forgets the symptoms
and the simulacra.
Blue-collar son
of blue-collar Scranton,
The President is lost in the ashes
of the 7-Elevens, the ashes
of the Walmarts and Targets.
"The peace of the world
has been preserved,
not by statesmen,
but by capitalists."[2]
How the mighty robber-barons,
the mighty men of steel
and rail and big-tech
and big-schemes,
how those mighty men
preserved our God-given

right to the land.
We listen for the penny
as we float down
the Columbia River.
We reached the Pacific
and the Corps of Discovery
listened for the ever-loving sploosh
as the copper entered
the salty wash.
The Corps of Discovery listened
and lost their way.
And the ashes of Mt. St. Helens
covered the world,
and the ashes of Mt. St. Helens
muffled any music that might
have bubbled over.
And Mt. St. Helens muffled
the silent song of those silent
falling pennies.
No sploosh in that briny,
briny deep.

II: Who Raised Those Totem Poles?

Staring into the vacuum
of St. Helens satori.
The osprey, the spotted sand-piper,
the barn-swallow,
they stare as they circle
that event horizon.
No light escapes the crater.
The sound of the falling penny
is trapped forever and for always.
Ash blew across the nation.
Cascade ash painted
the flurries of Michigan,
Ontario, Quebec
with a dusky sheen.
Pacific winds carried that plume
across the continent and into
our vivid elementary school
imaginations.
"Vancouver, Vancouver, this is it!"[3]
Vancouver, Vancouver,
you dropped your coins
into the fountains

of Pacific Center,
into the cascades of that Great
Columbia River,
and you clasped your hands
in hopeful prayer,
but the coins you dropped
into Louwala-Clough
were dropped in vain.
When Pahto and Wy'east
paddled down
that Great Columbia River,
as they sang "Roll on Columbia,
roll on" and chased the sunset,
they crossed the Bridge of the Gods.
They devastated the land,
the villages, the people,
and Loowit turned to stone.
Her life-breath now exhales
from the depths
of Mt. St. Helens,
but no penny ever
touched her soul.
And in the shadows
of the Cascade Range,
the Cowlitz raised their Totem Poles
to raise their roof-beams.
Raise high those roof beams,
and raise high the spirits
of old Northwest.
And leaving Puget Sound,
we leave the ever-falling penny
to its ever-falling doom.
And sacred Puget Sound
muffled the silent song
of those silent falling pennies.
And leaving Puget Sound,
we roll on to Weskan,
Sharon Springs, Topeka,
and all points east.

III: When Kansas Wept and Blew

Staring into the vacuum
of root-cellar satori.
Auntie Em, Hunk, Zeke,
Hickory bed down deep

with onions, carrots, potatoes,
sprouting but ready for stew.
They seek shelter as those
Kansas winds blow
across the Kansas waste.
They crucified mankind
on a cross of dust bowl blues,
but never shall they crucify
mankind on a cross of gold.[4]
"And you were there,
and you were there,
and you were there,"
as we gazed, with hands clenched
around that dust bowl penny,
at the sinking sun obscured
by the hot sands of
the Louisiana Purchase.
When Napoleon wept
on St. Helena
with his four cents an acre,
he knew his four cents
would never sound
the hollow knell upon hitting
the bedrock.
He knew there would be no
good-luck splash.
And there would be no
good-luck splash
as he hurled his twenty-franc piece
towards the shadows of
Lot's Wife,
he knew that the man
behind the curtain
would never send that Elban
fleet to free him again.
Marengo would never ride
through Flanders fields
to free him.
Trapped and forsaken,
Bonaparte called upon
his uerte monkeys,
his melting sorrows
and sang his melting songs
to the wind.
On St. Helena, Dorothy Gale,
with silver standard slippers,

sang too.
She sang as the winds blew.
She sang as the storm grew.
And cold Holcomb, Kansas
muffled the silent song
of those silent falling pennies.
She sang of the bluebirds
and rainbows
as the penny fell
from the towers
of that glowing
emerald city.

IV: The Halcion Days of Hernando

Staring into the vacuum
of Tampa Bay satori.
Sunshine Pier with anglers,
tourists, sharks, stingrays.
Grandma would cut my hair
on her back patio.
Sweeping it into the
gentle Florida breeze,
she said the seagulls
collected tufts to
pad their nests.
They padded nests
with hair and pennies.
The white birds keeping
their young warm within
the dark fluff and copper coins.
Supposedly, it's bad luck
to have your hair end up
in a nest,
but grandma never went
for superstition.
She stood on principle:
my utilitarian haircut helped
usher in the baby gulls
before they grew to beg
for scraps on those
white beaches of Tampa Bay.
They grew to soar above
The Sunshine Skyway,
to soar above the squall
that drove the Summit Venture

through the piers.
Cars, trucks, Greyhounds,
that second generation
Ford Courier, fell and sank.
All those pennies fell
and are still sinking today,
never reaching the floor
of the Gulf of Mexico.
Grandpa in the bed of
the pick-up, with stage make-up
and bandana, cutlass and hook:
those De Soto Days live on.
When my pirate hat
flew in the breeze
and my newly cut hair
was on display, I cried.
"Pirates don't cry," he told me.
"Pirates don't cry over lost hats
or falling pennies."
When those De Soto Days
muffled the silent song of
those silent falling pennies,
and all of those pennies of May
are still falling to this day.
And nothing copper can stay
when the Summit Venture
goes astray.

The Rue and the Swallowtail

The herb of grace
is grown with stately rose,
companions in the border
and the breeze.
Upon the golden rue
the swallowtail
will lay and feast
and grow to conquer all.
She flutters through
the garden on a beam
of sunlight
born to dance
in diamond June,
but come July
she's gone to distant shore.
Her fleeting nature
much the same as ours;
her momentary life's
eternal charm.

Hardy Mums of Autumn

The garden in late September
is dry and barren.
Often availing not,
we plant more mums
every year none-the-less.
The few that survive,
in yellows, oranges,
purples,
standing at attention
with the corn-stalk sentries,
the scarecrows,
the Jack-o-lanterns,
brighten the garden
when all else has
dimmed and
fallen.

Clear Walloon

To sleep the sleep of days,
cleansed by the water
of clear Walloon.
To sleep the amphibian
sleep of salamanders,
sirens and mudpuppies,
eyes shut tight like
The Annex doors on Sunday morning.
In a den of simplicity,
caring not for the big city
or the shadows in the dark,
caring not for Archduke Ferdinand
or trenches on the horizon.

To sleep the sleep of Milanese warfare.
To sleep the ambulatory sleep
of shell fragments, chocolate
and cigarettes.
The great tragedy still but a mirage
in the shadows
of Appennini and Po.
Camicie Nere of Piazza San Sepolcro
only a glimmer in the eye of Il Duce.
Asleep under the stars
of Bay Township,
under the boughs of aspen,
cedar, and hemlock.

The scent of burning birch
wafts through frozen teardrops
as unstuck lovers hide
in acid rain ashcans,
asleep perchance to scream.
Sleeping the still sad sleep
of Windemere Cottage.
Sleeping in the mill mad music
of malleability.
Down the banks he ran,
paddled across the western arm,
to fly through white pine
and sugar maple.

To sleep under stars
or in warm quilts of the Red Fox.

To cast and land with Vollie Fox,
and it is cold on the water,
and dying is pretty easy,
when you think on it.
"In the old days,
Horton Bay was a lumbering town."
To slumber in the lumber towns
of northern Michigan,
to sleep the wooden sleep
of Windemere and awaken
to the song of the nuthatch.

Course Catalogue Number LITR 207: An Archeology of the Giants of Latin America

"el muerte no es muerte: es la muerte."[1]

As Professor Stein started
her lecture,
I sat in the back,
quietly flying under
her radar.
She praised the genius
of every writer we covered,
but for some reason,
she stopped short with Borges.
She was holding something back.
It didn't make sense;
she loved Neruda
and Márquez,
Paz and even Fuentes.
She talked with such affection
about Love in the Time of Cholera,
One Hundred Years of Solitude,
Chronicles of a Death Foretold.
When quoting Neruda,
she closed her eyes and with raised,
shaking hands,
she transformed the room
into another world.
We were there
in that Santiago hospital.
We all raged against
Pinochet's needle.
For six and a half hours,
we watched him die.
Professor Stein took us there,
and it was beautiful.
"Love is so short,
forgetting is so long,"
she said, and we knew
what it was to die
at the hands of that
Chilean madman.

Borges was different though.
Years later, I learned
her secret.
She, too, had a piece of

that map.
Suárez Miranda
spelled it out so certainly.
The land was covered
and the land was the map.
Those cartographers
had left forgotten scraps behind
and in her silent journey
through the fallen kingdoms,
Professor Stein stumbled
upon the last vestiges of that
cartographic dream.
She never talked of it in class.
"Solitude is the profoundest fact
of the human condition," she told us.
In solitude
she clung to those ragged
pieces of history.
Eco claimed it impossible,
but she knew.
She held those depictions
of the empire close to her chest
as only a true believer could.
Not the reliefs only,
but also the artifacts and subjects.
She held them close
and remembered
the totality of killing time,
like Paz said, dying
"bit by bit."

Part IV: Dead Man's Hill

Radioactive Smiles

There is nothing to fear
in Aragón,
there is nothing to fear
in Catalonia.
There is nothing to fear
in the depths of
the Mariana Trench
but for the snailfish
and the deep-sea gigantism
of the amphipods.
In the pitch-black abyss,
the amphipods grow to
unreal size.
The amphipods will conquer
Tokyo, Seoul, Los Angeles
and the military will fire
rockets to no avail.
The military will detonate
the new Able
and the new Tsar Bomba.
A second coming of
Operation Crossroads
will lead us up those
Nirvanic steps.
They will lead us
to the ends of the atolls
with radiation sickness
and sly radioactive smiles.
But there is nothing to fear
in Aragón, and
there is nothing to fear
in Catalonia.

Icarus and the Rip Tide

The chimes of St. Francis
and the chimes of
clock towers
toll for the liars
and they toll
for the true.
There ain't no god in
Ypsilanti,
There ain't no soul
in Ypsilanti,
but Ypsilanti hearts
are open to all
tomorrow's cat naps.
All tomorrow's folly.
Ypsilanti hearts
are open to
inquiry and
Ukrainian cover-ups.

As the Amazon burns
and the ashes float
heavenward,
as the rainforest burns
and the ashes fall upon
Akuntsu faces
and Akuntsu feet,
they hear no chimes.
Akuntsu toes watch
the burning jungle night.
Kanoe and Akuntsu share
the scorched land, they
share a small meal.
The last meal of western
Amazonian famine.
The water runs bronze
with ochre mud
and the water runs
crimson with the falu
Akuntsu blood.
The Amazonian water
boils and churns
as flames eat
the honest wood.
Akutsu slice off ears

to ignore the chimes
of the church bells in
the distance.

The chimes of Hazlehurst
and the chimes
of Dockery toll
for the cotton pickers
and the cotton gin.
The Chimes of St. Francis
Sing out and pray
in the distance,
a thousand miles away.
The white cotton fluff
and the yellow wood
of guitars
shimmer in Mississippi sun.
The Delta mud
and the Delta warbler
shimmer and sing.
The song of
the prothonotary warbler
fills the air with
his twelve-bar blues
and his crossroad shuffle.
And the blues of
the warbler strum and toll
for the cotton pickers
and the cotton gin.

The chimes of St. Francis
toll for the work-a-day
brown shirt goose stepping
down Main St.
w/ a rifle on his shoulder
and a match
to *Leaves of Grass*.
"Books are the best
kindling," he says,
"because they send
their smoky images
soaring to the stratosphere,"
as he holds aloft
his rigid outstretched arm.
The calamus root tolls
for the blind-folded soldier,

up against the wall
and ready to fall
like autumn leaves
in brisk November wind.
Up against the wall,
mother fucker,
and fall like a stick
from the hand
of a boy on a
bridge.

The calamus root tolls
for Virginia Beach
and Bensonhurst
while Yusef Hawkins' blood
washes into the
East River,
out past Liberty Island,
out beyond Long Island Sound.
The lonesome lilac chimes
for the humpback swimming
from Long Island
to Vineyard Sound and
Nantucket.
And it chimes for
the young man from
Nantucket.

The children of Adam
toll and scream
for the children of Ham
and Canaan.
Their blood too washes
into the East River
and into the Mississippi River
and into the Okefenokee Swamp
and into the Bear River
starting from Charlevoix County
and ending at the
heels of St. Francis.
The drum taps
beat the rhythm of
the sinners and
the rhythm of police
force death.
Who among them

will tap the beat of
justice?
The chimes of St. Patrick's
Cathedral and the chimes of
the twin towers of Peter and Paul
toll for those fallen children,
but not for the fallow fields
or fine blue line.

The chimes of St. Francis
toll for the transients
and the chimes of
the clock towers
toll for the conscripts:
the conscripted youth
in fox-hole prison
sanctuaries eating
their atomic brunch.
Autumn is wasted on
the holocaust of youth.
The oblivious child
runs circles around the sun,
arms waving in ecstasy—
hop-scotching
into history books.

And there is a hole
above our heads.
The horizon weeps
as the orgone accumulator
becomes clogged
with the portrait of a passionate
woman and
the humors and elements
of earth and fire,
and backs up into
the throat of the laughing
midnight rain.
It backs up into
the storm drains
of Mother Russia.
Покро́вский собо́р bells
chime and fall
on bent ears.
The notes from the steeple
of St. Francis

escape through
the hole
and vanish into the void.
The chiming steeple bells
ring unnoticed
as the sweltering heat
of the 21st century
melts our eardrums.

And there is a hole
in the razor wire
surrounding the concentration
camps of our resilient hatred.
Inside a tooth falls
like the stick from the hand
of Christopher Robin
on a bridge.
Another tooth
and another.
Taste buds fall also,
never again to savor
the flavor.
Asleep in corners
without Rubin or
Doernberg
to hold them close
or ask of ice-cream.
Asleep in a cage
while they forget their
homeland and destination.
Asleep in the corners
of their cages
as the train whistle overcast
sky of December
herds them ever towards
disease and death.
A poem, too,
is an orgone accumulator
collecting the life force
and collecting the universe
and collecting the multiverse.
The chimes of St. Francis
toll for the strings
connecting us with
the holographic image
of the two-dimensional

borderline.
The chimes of the clock tower
toll for the dark matter
and the Higgs boson
as it creates and spirals
and decays.

We wear our waxy wings
as we glide, float,
sing towards
the old home place.
We wear our waxy
wings and fall from
grace.
We shed our waxy wings
as we splash down.
Huston, we have a problem;
Hustontown—
our splash-down ended
with neither glory nor
homecoming sash;
the undertow will carry
our blues away.
The undertow drags us
out to sea
passed Vineyard Sound
and the watery blood of
Pokrovsky Cathedral
and the watery blood of
Yusef Hawkins.

The darkest hour
is the hour of our youth.
The darkest hour
glows in the noon day sun,
while the moon reflects
the emotions of the lonesome
kettle of night.
And the chimes of St. Francis
toll deaf and dumb
for the wasted
holocaust of youth.

For a Child Who is Also a Cactus

Always on guard,
your spines are aimed
to protect and hide
your beauty.
Even in Michigan,
we've seen you
in the sandy fields
and the dunes of
Muskegon, Allegan,
Oceana.
Your yellow flower
lasts a day
and a day only,
but your honeyed fruit
quenches the long summer
afternoons.
In these dunes
we played and climbed.
In these dunes,
I carried you
with sand in your eyes.
Up and down, they trace
the old sand paths,
the old erosion.
They leap over your spiny pads
and never look back.
But you stand,
always on guard.
Always prepared to run.
Silently—prepared
to bury your head in your pillow
as we watch and weep.
As we are forever
at a loss for words.
As we are forever
saying the wrong thing.
Your spines only get you so far,
for you are also a
pin-cushion.
Poked and prodded by the
playground saguaro needles.

Your shallow roots,
always looking for a little water,

a connection so hard to find,
a connection to fill your pads
and hydrate your ripe
fragrant bloom,
in the desert of schoolyard pain.
Reaching and reaching,
but shell-shocked
and alone.

Opuntia blossom
in the sands of youth
and the wasteland of
forgotten silence.
The child
who is also a
cactus

who is also a
pin-cushion

who is also
a

jewel.

When Stars Fade

If a picture contains
the possibility of the smokescreen
that it represents,
and if sending unsolicited dick-pics
to JD Vance is in line
with God's work,
and if jumping for joy
as the candy cigarettes' chalky dust/ash
collects on the tongues
of loafers, sneakers,
and saddle shoes
is within the purview of
Neptune and Apollo,
and if braless young women
paint their faces like butterflies
or Wonder Woman,
and if we stand and cross out hearts
and mouth the words to
The Battle of Fort McHenry,
then all the stars might
fall at once
and all the stars might fade.

She Brings the Winter

She brings the winter
on her wings
and rides the stardust
The winter wind
blows home the heart
The winter wind
shines softly

She brings the winter wind
on wings of smoke
and mirrors.
The wind blows
sweetly through
silent days of
silent songs

She cries in winter bed
as snow-blind
seasons fall
The seasonal tears
drive home the wind
And her tears
drown the snow.

Brunchtime of the Idols

> "Inmitten einer düstern und über die Maassen
> verantwortlichen Sache seine
> Heiterkeit aufrecht erhalten
> ist nichts Kleines von—Kunststück:
> und doch, was wäre nöthiger als
> Heiterkeit?" [1]

When the thunderstorm
is frozen in the sky
and the farmhouse
is spinning, spinning
through spectral sounds
of the coming calm,
we bid good evening
to forgotten kings
and the gods of the Oregon Trail.
Only there in the valley
of the great rolling Missouri
will we find the ruts
of the covered wagon.
Independence Rock,
carved with the names
of those forgotten pioneers,
rises in the distance,
and we find the ruts
of the covered wagons.
The ruts of those old wheels
cut deep into the mud
and deep into the heart of the
land.
In soar arrows
from the mighty Sioux,
the Pawnee, the Arapaho.
Shoshone warriors
burn the camps,
hunt the great bison.
The bison herd fills the horizon.
The bison herd
runs free in
circles, zig zags,
start and stop glory.
The bison head hung
on the supermarket wall
eyeing the butcher and
the baker.

When the lightening
is blotted out of the heavens
by a host of the shiniest cherubim,
and the farmhouse
is crashing, crashing
on amber waves of pain,
we bid a fond farewell
to the gods of the Oregon Trail.
In the canyon of
the Little Colorado,
we saw the lizard lose
its tail and scream.
We bought turquoise slides
for our bolo ties
and we rode the black horse,
Toronado,
as we carved our Z's
into the mythology of Route 66.
And the gods of
the Snow Cap Drive-in
nestled into a booth
for a long afternoon of
checkers, backgammon,
solitaire, whist.
In soar the pebbles kicked up
by tires of the Desoto Adventurer,
the Studebaker Power Hawk,
the AMC Rambler.
The Plymouth Furies burn rubber,
hunt birds up and down
Thunder Road.
On Thunder Road,
Robert Mitchum died
rounding the curve near
Kingston Pike.
The ghost of Robert Mitchum
runs free in circles, zig zags,
start and stop glory.
The ghost of Robert Mitchum
wanders the aisles
eyeing the grocery girls
and planning a midnight run.

When the hail
is hammering the tarmac
and the farmhouse flies

diagonally, diagonally
into the future of next year's
autumnal equinox,
we say good day to
Baron von Aurantiaco
and the gods of the Oregon Trail.
Walking the canyon streets
of New York, Detroit,
Washington D.C.,
we felt the sleet hammer
us too.
November turns December,
we turn our collar to the wind
and rain.
We climbed the Empire State Building
one step at a time,
1,576 stairs,
and the observation deck
was bursting with tourist fluff
and the twenty-five-cent binocular stands
were out of order.
No blimps moored that day either.
In soar the tourists
to gentrify and spend.
The Chrysler, The Penobscot,
The Washington Monument
hidden on the horizon
as the gods of the National Mall
patted themselves on the back
and said, "Well done, brothers."
And Jack Ruby
runs free in circles, zig zags,
start and stop glory,
saying, "Look on my works,
ye foolish,
and eat well,"
eying the pickles and olives.

When the fog
fills the farmhouse
and the river valley quakes
shivering, shivering
as tectonic plates
collide, we sing
"Auld Lang Syne"
with an invisible choir

of Disney princesses
as the Gods of the Oregon Trail
are lost to hazy
yesteryear.
Exploring Big Thunder
Mountain, Tom Sawyer's Island,
Spaceship Earth,
we look for mouse-eared
water to quench our
central Florida thirst.
Remembering Tomorrowlands
of childhood bliss,
climbing Space Mountain
as slippery hands grip
the bar and we fly
through the dark.
No more can we spy
Goofy or the Country Bears
as they have all
gone home.
They're tucked in their
warm beds for the night.
They've supped on
gruel and butterscotch;
they've supped on the misfortunes
of the alligator infested
central Florida swamps.
The tourist herds
floods the horizon,
and the ghost of John Mills
swings through the branches
in circles, zig zags,
start and stop glory,
singing his song,
"That's the quarantine flag...
I do a bit of reading too,
you know,"[2]
into the wild zebra night.

Lord Buckley, Lord Buckley

Lord Buckley was born
down in Tuolumne County
with the Tuolumne jingle
and the walk of a
priest.
Lord Buckley was singin',
"Hezekiah, Hezekiah"
to an audience of
noblemen
and an audience of fools.
Nobody knows
who the bad guy is.
Nobody knows the
Creeper.
In the deep open plains
of Canadian tundra
and northern coniferous
forests,
the spirit of
Lord Buckley haunts
the arctic fox.
The spirit of
Lord Buckley haunts
the polar bear,
the pinniped,
the muskox.

And there was a cat,
the Nazz.
Look at that cat go.
Nobody knows the Nazz.
Look at that Nazz
lay it down.
You know,
when Lord Buckley said
the Nazz laid it down,
Lord Buckley said it
stayed down.
And when the Nazz
walked on water,
he didn't drown.

Cast down your nets
on the flip side.

Cast down your buckets
where you're at.
Cast down your
filth and funk.
Cast it down into the
depths of Lord Buckley's
complete oeuvre.
Grab hold of Lord Buckley's
little Lord Buckley
and ride it like the wind.
And run like the wind,
Bullseye...
run like the wind.

Lord Buckley fought
the Battle at Jericho,
and the walls came
tumbling down.
Lord Buckley fought
the Battle of the Alamo,
while Tejanos,
to the last man,
remained in his thoughts.
With his long rifles
and his twelve-pound guns,
Lord Buckley stood
with the Tejanos.
He sent three cannon
to Goliad,
left a twenty-one gun
salute
for Santa Anna, de Cos,
and their boys.
And as Santa Anna
and de Cos
and their boys
stormed the walls,
Lord Buckley sang,
"Farewell to the Mountains,
farewell to them all."

Westward Expansion
and Manifest Destiny
and Lord Buckley
rowed and walked
and crawled

through Napoleonic lands
while the girl, Sacagawea,
the warrior, Sacagawea
rowed and walked
and crawled
with him.
Pregnant with purpose
and large with child,
she rowed and walked and crawled
with Lord Buckley
to find the Pacific Ocean.
The Shoshone woman
and the Tuolumne Lord
led the Corps of Discovery,
the Corps of Science
and Death,
to Missouri head-waters
and Columbia cascades.

And there was a cat,
the Nazz.
Look at that cat go.
Nobody knows the Nazz.
Look at that Nazz
lay it down.
You know,
when Lord Buckley said
the Nazz laid it down,
Lord Buckley said it
stayed down.
And when the Nazz
walked on water,
he didn't drown.

Lord Buckley Lord Buckley
killed poor Mr. Lincoln
and the poor folks
in Ford Theater
watched his poor
head explode.
He yelled
"Death to all tyrants"
and jumped from
the rafters
and ran from the balcony
and sat by the

fire
to warm his
sore feet.
And when Mr. Kennedy
fell back to the left,
Lord Buckley, Lord Buckley
he watched from the
shadows
like he hid in the shadows
of the Women's Waiting Room
on 2 July 1881
and flew from the barrel
and embedded in
Mr. Garfield's chest,
and said "Chester shall
be my president
for I am a stalwart."

Lord Buckley
was crushed under 4,000 hooves
as the armies rode down
from the top of the hill.
And Lakota warriors
drove invading doom
from the land of
the pregnant Sacagawea
and the Black Hills
of picnic tomorrow.
Those Lakota warriors
Drove the purpose of corrosion
and empire from the Black Hills.
Lord Buckley was born
down in Tuolumne County
with the Tuolumne jingle
and the walk of a priest.
And when Lord Buckley
walked on water,
he didn't drown.

A Fistful of Ennui

As the Sergio Leone score
floats through
the Mall of America
and we collectively
price ourselves out of
a new pair of Jordans,
we bow our heads
and tuck our thumbs
into our "Keep on Truckin'"
belt buckles.
Few can recall how
far she fell
down, down, down
before she lodged
in a West Texas well-casing.
Baby Jessica sang her songs.
Baby Jessica sang
"Winnie the Pooh,
Winnie the Pooh,
chubby little cubby
all stuffed with fluff,"
and the world sang with her,
but she wasn't
all stuffed with fluff.
She lost a toe to gangrene
and we lost our innocence
to the covers of People Magazine,
Time, Redbook.
And to the stories in The Daily News,
The Washington Post,
and The Petoskey News Review.

As "The Love Theme from
Switchblade Sisters"
floated through the halls
of the Satellite of Love,
we wore our Nikes
and waited for redemption
behind Hale-Bop.
When the UFO arrived,
we boarded with
our utter anxiety
and our silly dreams.

If Nike only manufactured
clown shoes,
we would have been
the perfect emblem of
democracy.
The sign relationship as a whole,
flying around the sun
and back to the icy darkness
of the solar system.
While Hale-Bop glowed
in the northwest sky,
we knew salvation
was at hand.

As "We Built this City"
floated through
the bowling alleys,
pool halls, video arcades
of our junior high blues,
we had them ol' junior high
blues again, mama,
and we filled our void
with quarters for Galaga,
Pole Position, Q*Bert,
the chill of Northern Michigan
returned;
we pulled our faux fur collars
close around our necks.
Thank God it's Thinsulate.
Our ears, red with frostbite,
listened intently for distant
signs of agency.
While Q*Bert forever fell
from his pyramid,
we fell too.
We toppled towards
The Bear River rush
and towards that frozen
water wonderland.

Rosedale

I
Starting from Westchester,
New Rochelle & Hartsdale
Tuckahoe & Tarrytown,
In theaters & on streets,
We carried the garbage to the
dumpster together,
We sat by the pool.
Two long winters
& a flight to Florida.
Coca Cola visions of
Marshall McLuhan
& Kenneth Burke.
Poetry as symbolic action.

At the Christian Brothers School,
Down a blind street,
You fought the good fight,
Certa Bonum
Certamen.
Off, off Broadway,
Certa Bonum
Certamen.

Empire State Building,
Home of King Kong
& Schenley,
World Trade Center
Tappan Zee
Staten Island Ferry &
Lincoln Tunnel:
The Bohemian life in Manhattan.
Black & white images w/
shadow & grace.
Pitchers of pilsner
w/ students & colleagues.
Fourth of July picnics
w/ burgers & brats.
You smoked your pipe,
played chess
& read.
Beethoven on the record player,
you smoked your pipe,
played chess

& read.

& you were the proud
father.

Day trips to
The Cloisters & Coney Island,
Bryant Park & The Gaslight,
Village Gate & Café Wha?
Ali's Alley & Eddie Condon's.
Gene Krupa played
& the standing room crowd
spilled onto the
sidewalk.
Grandpa was so impressed.

Haldeman has what ITT takes.
Ehrlichman & Mitchell
conspired
while you smoked your pipe &
memorized
Bach, Tennessee Williams,
Brendan Behan.

No bricks thrown at you though.
Held hostage on the Hudson,
You were the proud father;
You sought refuge in the
Charlevoix snow.

II
Starting from Windcrest,
1976,
we walked to the General Store
& the Post Office.
"Who is that masked man?"
they asked.
"Who has arrived w/ such
time on his hands?"
We walked the trails
behind the old high school
picking morels & getting lost.

One morel,
big as my foot,
grew under a white pine.

It went in the marinara.
Collecting wild leeks
Behind the house—
They went in the marinara

Conversations w/ Ray
at the marina.
Outboard engines &
The mine waters of Quecreek.
Conversations w/ Ray,
Who introduced you to your next,
best mania.
Loquunter cum
pedibus,
a sturdy defender,
Loquunter cum
pedibus,
we traveled to
Boyne City, Harbor Springs, etc.
We ate DQ Starkiss
as the giant biker's classic trike
backfired.
& the bikers partied on the shore
as Budweiser pop-tops
littered the
grass
by the headwaters of
the Bear River.

& you were the proud
father.

Sunny sat on her front porch,
Shotgun loaded w/
Rock-salt.
"Get off my land"
she yelled,
tired of reporters looking
for loot,
looking for stories of her
brother,
& she fired passed our heads.
"Don't shoot, Sunny!"
you shouted.
as we approached the cottage.

& you were the proud
father.

Producing plays
at the Dilworth.
Bats in the belfry
during The Glass Menagerie,
w/ the suit of armor
made from the old
stove pipes.
This Property is Condemned.
The Dilworth, too,
was condemned.
You wrote one about Penn/Dixie.
"Can you get my son a job?"
The irony never lost
on the audience.

& you were the proud
father.

III
Starting from Walloon,
1978,
MASH & Happy Days
Rockford & Hogan.
With Rick, you dove
into the arena.
On the roof,
you adjusted the antenna
watching matches
from Canada.
Soccer Saturdays
& Mothers' Days
In the van, you saw Midland
& Sault Ste. Marie
& Canton. Livonia
& the Zilwaukee Bridge.

You showed us
Your childhood in
Rosedale.
Swimming pool
& Catholic school
& bus rides through Detroit.

Van rides through America
to Everglades, Smoky Mountains,
Acadia National Park.
Ferry from Bar Harbor to
Nova Scotia,
from lobster lunch
to living history.
Crepes & fresh
baguette from those
roadside ovens.
Whales sounding off
the coast
as we rounded
the cliffs
toward Quebec City
cathedral
& Montreal
playground.

Reagan & Weinberger
Poindexter & North
sold guns
for hostages &
we saw you on
weekends
after the drive
down I 75.
We missed you
for a year
& then moved
south.

IV
Starting from Wayne
County, 1988.
Canton & Hanford Rd.
We watched Pink
Panther films &
Old SNL episodes.
Letterman & Seinfeld.
You stood in the
blizzard
watching the meets.
Watching other kids
race down slopes
of ice and artificial snow.

A proud father
without a horse
in the race.

With vertigo & bad knees
you started
showing your age.
With money problems &
depression
you started
showing your age.
You were half asleep
& I was stoned
in your sister's
basement after school:
MST3K on the television,
but you were able
to move on & up.
Back to Canton
& Eurorails with
King Kirby.

You showed us
the Penobscot & Fischer
Guardian & One Detroit,
Greek Town, Cork Town,
fireworks, & Thanksgiving
football.
We saw the glass eye
silhouetted against the
setting Comerica Park
sun.

With bottomless glass
of Cabernet,
you sang Sinatra & Elvis,
"Hey Jude" &
"What a Wonderful
World."

You were the proud
grandfather.
Through cancer
& knee replacement,
you were the proud
grandfather.

Road-trips &
aerodynamic flapjacks,
movie theaters
& sushi.

You were the proud
grandfather.

Night of the Murdered Poets

"Perhaps these aren't poetic times at all"
Nikki Giovanni

I wanted to write a poem
about Minneapolis.
I wanted to write a poem
about the murder of
Renee Nicole Good,
but I didn't know
where to start.

Maybe I should start
on 9 November 1938
when a German diplomat
was assassinated in Paris,
and the assassin happened
to be Jewish.
In response, the SS along
with the SA and members
of the Hitler Youth destroyed
1,400 synagogues
and 7,000 Jewish owned businesses.
Hitler's government turned a blind eye.
Hitler's government, in fact,
encouraged it.
In the aftermath,
and I mean within two days
of the pogrom,
within two days of that
Night of Broken Glass,
30,000 Jewish men were rounded up
and sent to camps:
Buchenwald, Dachau, and Sachsenhausen.
The government used this
as an excuse to further the detainment
and murder of the Jewish community
throughout Germany, Austria,
and the Sudetenland.
They used it as an excuse
to seize land and wealth.

Or maybe I should start
in September of 1948
when the Soviet government
began arresting Jewish activists.

By June of 1949
Thirteen men had been detained.
Thirteen men never to be seen again.
These men, these proud members
of a society that never wanted them,
were falsely accused
of espionage and terrorism.
They sat in prison for three years,
during which they were
beaten, tortured, and raped.
This culminated in August of 1952
with their murders.
On 12 August 1952,
The Night of the Murdered Poets,
all thirteen men were assassinated
in their cells, in Lubyanka Prison.
That prison still stands.
With proper approval,
you can even visit it.
You can tour the cells, the toilets,
the museum.
That prison still stands,
but those thirteen men
fell that night,
never to stand again.
Businessmen, government officials,
politicians, scientists,
and five brave poets
were never to stand again.

Or maybe I should start
In October of 1968.
Students from across
Mexico City had organized.
Students from across
Mexico City stood up to
the Partido Revolucionario Institucional.
The nationalistic, authoritarian
government, backed by
Lyndon Baines Johnson
and the United States,
moved on the demonstrators.
The nationalistic, authoritarian government,
with American weapons and American funds,
was preparing for the Olympics,
was afraid of the bad press

before the Olympics,
was in need of a quick solution.
That solution came
on 2 October 1968
as the troops entered
Plaza de las Tres Culturas
and opened fire.
Thousands were arrested,
thousands were injured,
and hundreds, with the hearts of poets,
lay dead in the square,
murdered by the US backed
Partido Revolucionario Institucional
to ensure a successful Summer Olympics.

Or maybe I should start
in September of 1973.
That's when Pablo Neruda
was suffering with prostate cancer.
That's when Pablo Neruda
was on his deathbed
in a Santiago hospital;
he was nearing the end.
Pinochet couldn't wait though.
Pinochet needed his death expedited.
On 23 September 1973,
Pinochet tasked a doctor
with the strangest of jobs:
injecting poison into Neruda's stomach.
Perhaps the most famous poet
ever assassinated
Was assassinated by his
authoritarian government.
"Tonight, I can write the saddest lines" he said.
Tonight, in the wake of Renee Nicole Good,
we can all write the saddest lines.
I've read his poems.
I've known that the life of a poet
could be dangerous.
Neruda showed us
that the life of a poet
could, in fact, be deadly.

Or maybe I should start
in June of 1989.
That's when, after months of protests

following the death of Hu Yaubang,
students gathered in Beijing.
Demanding justice, equality, free elections,
students gathered in Beijing.
A peaceful protest,
labeled a "Counter-Revolutionary Rebellion"
in official government statements,
and soon labeled simply as a "riot,"
was broken up by the military.
You see, 300,000 troops from
The People's Liberation Army
were deployed to Beijing.
300,000 troops to quell the uprising.
By the morning of 4 June 1989
3,000 people, poets to the last,
were dead in Tiananmen Square.
By the morning of 4 June 1989,
3,000 people had been murdered
by a scared government
that knew the winds of change
were blowing.

Did you know Renee Nicole Good
was a poet? Did you know
she was a human being?
Kristi Noem called her a
"Domestic terrorist."
Donald Trump has doubled down,
calling her "disorderly."
He claimed she "violently, willfully,
and viciously ran over
the ICE Officer."
Joseph Goebbels said,
"The bigger the lie,
the more they believe it."
Hitler's Minister of Propaganda
alive and well in The Department
of Homeland Security,
alive and well in The Oval Office.
Noem claimed Good a domestic terrorist
even though we've all seen the videos,
even though we've all stared in disbelief
as our screens showed us the murder
over and over again.

She wasn't killed because she was a poet.
She wasn't killed because she was a mother.
She wasn't killed because she was Jewish, or Christian, or Muslim.
She wasn't killed because she was a beloved family member.
She was killed because the ICE Officer fucked up.
She was killed because we've allowed poorly trained thugs to patrol our streets.
Almost five years to the day after the treasonous January Sixth insurrection,
she was killed because she was in the wrong place at the wrong time.
She was killed because our government,
like the Soviets, the Nazis,
the Partido Revolucionario Institucional,
the Pinochet regime,
The Communist Party of China,
is afraid.

She was murdered by a fucking piece of shit.
On 7 January 2026, she was murdered.

Notes

In the Arena of the Alligator:
1. Rouse, Ervine T. "Orange Blossom Special." 1938.

Gaspé Peninsula:
1. Fréchette, Louis Honoré. "La Voix d'un Exilé." 1868.

Boxing the Compass:
1. Kazantzakis, Nikos. *Zorba the Greek*. Translated by Carl Wildman. Scribner, 1981. P 121. Catalogue Course Number: LITR 207:
1. Borges, Jorge Luis. "Remorse for Any Death." Line 3.

Waiting for the Sploosh:
1. Wise, Alana. "No Excuse for Looting: Biden, Trump Respond to Philadelphia Protests." NPR. 28 October 2020. https://www.npr.org/2020/10/28/928761401/no-excuse-for-the-looting-biden-trump-respond-to-philadelphia-protests

2. Disraeli, Benjamin. Qtd. in *The Life of Benjamin Disraeli*, Earl of Beaconsfield vol. 4.1855-1868. William Flavelle Moneypenny and George Earle Buckle, authors. Forgotten Books, 2018.

3. Johnson, David. Qtd. In "Vancouver, Vancouver, This is It." Sally Ousley, author. *Corvallis Gazette Times*. 17 May 2020. https://www.gazettetimes.com/news/local/ uerte er-vancouver-this-is-it/article_a1cfc433-1c5f-5c43-856c-772459fe831d.html

4. Bryan, William Jennings. "The Cross of Gold Speech." Delivered at The Democratic National Convention, Chicago, IL, 9 July 1896.

Brunchtime of the Idols:
1. Nietzsche, Freidrich. *Twilight of the Idols*. 1889.

2. Mills, John. *The Swiss Family Robinson*. Walt Disney Productions. 1960.

Acknowledgments

In the Arena of the Alligator appeared in *Resurrection Magazine*

West of Texarkana and Blind Alleyways of Yesteryear appeared in *Alternate Route*

Joshua Tree appeared in *The Elevation Review*

See Rock City appeared in *The Elevation Review*

Down the Barbed Wire Highway appeared in *About Place*

Across Pigeon Key appeared in *The Amphibian Literary Magazine*

Above New River Gorge appeared in *Apricot Press*

Gaspé Peninsula appeared in *Resurrection Mag*

Leave Only Mufflers Appeared in *Skyway Journal*

Someone Else's Stars appeared in *The Write Launch*

Still Life w/ Locomotives appeared in *Lothlorien Poetry Journal*

Goodnight, Taj Mahal appeared in *Gnashing teeth*

Robben Island Beach Break and Radioactive Smile appeared in *Pop the Culture Pill*

Bristlecone Soul appeared in *Pinehills Review*

Out Cimarron Way appeared in *DoubleSpeak*

Gagarin in the Trees appeared in *Sienna Solstice*

She Showed Me Her Scars appeared in *Corporeal Magazine*

Uncle Ebeneezer/Uncle Stockhausen and Icarus and the Rip Tide appeared in *Cerasus*

Boxing the Compass appeared in *The Field Guide*

Upside-Down Skies appeared in *Tofu Ink*

The Center of Gravity appeared in *Discretionary Love*

Waiting for the Sploosh appeared in *Menacing Hedge*

The Rue and the Swallowtail appeared in *Eucalyptus and Rose Literary Magazine*

Clear Walloon appeared in *Lion and Lilac*

Course Catalogue Number LITR 207 appeared in *La Piccioletta Barca*

Our Azure Earth appeared in *Lothlorien Poetry Journal*

For a Child Who is Also a Cactus appeared in *Quillkeepers*

Brunchtime of the Idols appeared in *Menacing Hedge*

A Fistful of Ennui appeared in *Sixfold*

Lord Buckley, Lord Buckley appeared in *Open Work*

Rosedale appeared in *Vermilion Press*

Thanks to Wyrd Byrd, Schuler's Books, Leopard Print Books, Sidetrack Bookshop, Quimby's, 27th Letter Books, and all of the small, independent booksellers and all of the presses who have also supported me like Alien Buddha, Back Room, and Finishing Line. Finally, a big thanks to the Eastern Michigan University Department of English and Literature, and of course, my parents, my kids (Solstice, Aiden, Isaiah, and Hugo), and my Bond Girl, my awesome partner in crime, Sara (Ms. Rizor if you're nasty).

Special thanks Carlton Ridenhour, Kris Parker, Tim Fielder, Melanie M. Goodreaux-Fielder, Deirdre Fagan, Fred Shrum III, Spike Lee, All the lads from Forest Verde FC, The Arsenal of North London, Patti Smith, Kevin Smith, Bob Dylan, Herbie Hancock, Steve Amick, Annie Ernaux, David McClendon (spelled w/ an "M" not a "D"), Dan Moyer, Jason Duerr (still fragile after all these years), Jeff Bean (Mr. Bean keeps it clean), Gina, Jess, Stephanie.

Extra Special thanks to Daisy for protecting me from the Amazon guy and keeping my feet warm, Dr. Watson and Mrs. Hudson: the best red-eared sliders this side of the Mississippi, Sarge and Penny: the cutest kittens of all time, and all the small journals and indie bookstores who have supported me over the last few years.

Super Double thanks in memory of Walt Whitman, Frederick Douglass, Virginia Woolf, Alex Raymond, William S. Burroughs, Nikki Giovanni, Jerry Garcia, Ida B. Wells, Ishiro Honda, Phil Lesh, Nina Simone, Miles Davis, John Coltrane, Lauren Bacall, Bogie, William S. Burroughs, Bob Kane, Bill Finger, Stan Lee, Jack Kirby, Virginia Woolf, Roberto Bolaño, Allen Ginsberg, Davy Crockett, Jacques Derrida, and my old man: Gary F. Peltier.

On the Strength: All the good folks at Wyrd Byrd, Ziggy's, and The Tap Room, Shawn Gates (do not feed hallucinogens to the werewolves), Christina Kallery (Tommy Wiseau will love you forever), Ken MacGregor, Tom Zimmerman, Tom Ulch (lock and load, mother fucker or better yet, charge et verrouille, fils de pute), Matt Kirkpatrick, Lisa Bennington-Love, Felicia MacArthur, Tommy Cook (keep laughing, baby!), Cal Freeman, R. J. Fox, Alison Swan, Sean Madigan Hoen, and Tom Barton.

This volume is set in the Aptos typeface.

www.ingramcontent.com/pod-product-compliance
Lightning Source LLC
La Vergne TN
LVHW090534110826
845146LV00003B/1090